Avoiding a

TRUCKING
NIGHTMARE

WHAT YOU **NEED** TO KNOW
After a Truck-related Injury

PATRICK CUMMINGS

Shannon Law Group
A Professional Corporation

Shannon Law Group, P.C.

Chicago Office
135 S. LaSalle, Suite 2200
Chicago, Illinois 60603

Woodridge Office
3550 Hobson Road, Suite 403
Woodridge, Illinois 60517

www.shannonlawgroup.com

Tel: 312.578.9501
Fax: 312.268.5474
Email: pcummings@shannonlawgroup.com

Designed and published by

Word Association Publishers
205 Fifth Avenue
Tarentum, Pennsylvania 15084

www.wordassociation.com
1.800.827.7903

CONTENTS

FOREWORD

JOSEPH P. SHANNON

SHANNON LAW GROUP, P.C.

Our clients' lives have been permanently shattered by transportation companies who do not have the proper safety mechanisms in place to ensure that its drivers and their rigs are safe for the roadways. Since I started working as a trial lawyer in 1988, I have worked on truck crash cases. Over those decades of work, I have come to understand that each crash has a backstory to explain why this type of tragedy occurred. It's our job to uncover the real facts as to why this tragedy happened to our clients.

Since he began his career at SLG six years ago, Patrick Cummings has been in the trenches in these battles. You want Patrick in your corner because he refuses to be intimidated by big trucking companies, their insurance companies, or their army of lawyers ... ever. His zealous advocacy for our clients, tremendous work ethic, and brilliant strategies have helped our clients find out why their lives were forever changed. As a direct result of Patrick's work, our clients now have a lifetime of financial security.

This book reveals some of the common factors in a trucking case. It is our hope that you find this book useful to you and your family as you tackle the big struggle that lies ahead.

DISCLAIMER

This book is informative in nature. It does not constitute legal advice.

If you need legal advice, please follow the advice in this book to find and retain an attorney. Only an attorney fully apprised of the particular facts of your situation can provide the legal advice you need.

The laws applicable to trucking crashes can vary from state to state. Where the information in this book is Illinois-specific, I point that out. Otherwise, this advice is generally applicable throughout the United States.

Included in this book are some examples and stories from actual cases I have tried or on which I worked. To protect the privacy of those involved, the names and identifying details have been changed.

Finally, this book is in no way a rebuff of the trucking industry or truck drivers. The vast majority of truck drivers are skilled, hardworking employees trying to provide for their families. As in any industry, there is a small percentage of bad actors that take shortcuts or put profits ahead of safety. These bad actors often cause serious and needless truck crashes that hurt the reputation of the industry and truck drivers as a whole.

INTRODUCTION

When I was a kid and people asked me, "What do you want to be when you grow up?", I never once told someone that I wanted to be a trucking attorney. In high school, as I was beginning to apply to colleges, I was forced for the first time to consider what I wanted to do with my life. Even then, becoming a trucking attorney wasn't close to my radar.

My seventeen-year-old self probably would have predicted that I would become a writer of some sort. When I wasn't shooting hoops or firing up a game of wiffleball with my friends, I spent a lot of my youth reading and writing stories. During my childhood, I fell in love with storytelling. In the midst of the Chicago Bulls 1990s glory days, I would record full-length radio broadcasts of Bulls games that happened entirely in my head. Somewhere in my parents house is a box of cassette tapes filled with "Michael kicks it to Harper on the wing. Harper drives to the middle, passes to Scottie. And Scottie DUNKS on Barkley!"

Every opportunity I had to take a creative writing class or just share my stories with class-mates, I leapt at the opportunity. For two years in junior high at St. Joan of Arc, I published the bi-weekly "Pat's News" (later re-branded as the more mature sounding Thursday Tribune) chronicling the important SJA news of the day, from my sixth grade football season to in-depth coverage of our gym class's badminton championship match.

By the time I graduated Marquette, I still hadn't commit-ted (or considered) a career as a trucking attorney. At that time, I wasn't sure what I wanted to do. Ultimately, I followed in my father's footsteps and went to law school. When I started working as a law clerk for Joe Shannon during my last year in law school, I still hadn't bound myself to any particular area of the law. In fact, had I not clerked at Shannon Law Group that spring, I probably would have ended up working for the public defender's office representing the criminally accused. I enjoyed the idea of being the only person in someone's corner against the endless resources of the government. Representing individuals charged with crimes would have allowed me the opportunity to tell their stories to judges and juries.

When I started clerking at SLG, I had my own idea of what civil litigation was, and I could not have been more wrong. In my mind, civil litigation and personal injury law in particular primarily involved groveling with insurance companies, beg-ging them to offer money to clients. And while some personal injury firms subscribe to that model of resolving cases, I quickly learned that Shannon Law Group operates very differently. We are not a settlement mill firm – we are trial lawyers. What that meant for me is that every day I have the opportunity to tell my clients' stories, and not to insurance adjusters – but to an actual audience, a jury of twelve people. Once I realized that, I was hooked on this area of the law. For my entire legal career, I've had the tremendous opportunity and honor to represent injured victims and to make sure that their story is heard.

* * * * *

On a cold February several years ago, Catherine[1] was driving her Toyota Prius to her dentist's office on a suburban county road not far from a busy expressway. About a half mile before the entrance ramp onto the expressway, Catherine had to travel through a traffic light-controlled intersection. As she was passing through the intersection, a roadside service truck made a left-hand turn and t-boned Catherine's car. It was a massive impact.

Catherine's driver side door was crunched into the body of the car. She was trapped inside. Emergency personnel had to use the Jaws of Life to extricate her from the wreckage. Catherine sustained life-altering crush injuries to the entire left side of her body and her spine. She underwent seven surgeries, hundreds of physical therapy sessions and incurred a mountain of medical bills. For the next two-and-a-half years, she would be confined to hospitals, rehabilitation facilities and nursing homes. This formerly independent woman could no longer take care of herself; she could no longer live on her own at home.

---

1   Throughout this book I share stories from some of my cases that demonstrate the importance of choosing a good lawyer for your trucking case. I have changed my clients' names to protect their anonymity.

Did the trucking company that t-boned Catherine accept responsibility for the tremendous damage that their driver caused? Of course not. At her deposition about a year after the crash, the truck driver testified under oath that she had turned on a green arrow, and that our client must have blown through a red light – thus causing her own injuries. Making the situation murkier, Catherine had sustained a brain injury that left her with no memory of the crash and no ability to refute the testimony of the driver.

Fortunately, our team's investigation revealed that the driver's story hadn't always been so black and white. In fact, in her written statement from the day of the crash, she said she thought she might have had a green turn arrow, but she wasn't sure. When she appeared in traffic court, the truck driver stipulated the facts as written on the police report by the investigating officer (which stated she failed to yield to on-coming traffic while turning on a *straight* green light). When our investigator contacted her a couple weeks after the crash, the truck driver said she never saw Catherine's car until the moment of impact. She believed that Catherine was on the other side of a slight hill when she started her turn. According to the driver, Catherine must have sped into the intersection so fast that she arrived in the intersection before the truck driver could finish her turn. As our accident reconstructionist explained, Catherine would have had to be traveling *252 miles per hour in a Prius* for the truck driver's sequence of events to be true.

Our investigation wasn't done once we thought we had a grasp on WHAT happened in this crash. Next, we had to figure out WHY. After taking the depositions of the driver and the trucking company's "safety personnel," it became clear that the company did not do any vetting of the driver before hiring her. If they had, they would have realized that the nineteen-year-old driver had only had her regular driver's license for about four months before hiring. They would have also learned that in that short driving history, the driver had two "serious" driving violations including a citation for drag-racing on a busy suburban road. After being confronted with that information, the owner of the trucking company testified that he never would have hired the driver if he had known of her history of reckless driving – something the rules required him to find out about before hire. Unfortunately for our client, this admission was far too late to prevent her catastrophic injuries.

With trucking cases, there's typically more to the story than appears at first glance. Trucking

As our accident reconstructionist explained, Catherine would have had to be traveling *252 MILES PER HOUR IN A PRIUS* for the truck driver's sequence of events to be true.

companies in America are governed by hundreds of specific rules and regulations geared towards making their operations safe. You see, operating heavy tractor-trailers is dangerous business. In exchange for allowing interstate trucking companies to make money operating trucks, the federal government requires the company to guarantee that it will operate according to the safety rules put in place by federal law. These guarantees are akin to a social contract -- a promise to the government and the motoring public that the company will play by the safety rules. When these companies do not follow the rules or remain willfully ignorant of their obligations, they break their promise.

There are hundreds of small, usually underfunded trucking companies that do not make safety a priority. These trucking companies ignore the promises they made to the federal government and the public in general by routinely hiring unqualified truck drivers that have no business being behind the wheel of a big rig. Those unqualified drivers share the road with all of us for millions of miles every year. The unsafe companies like the one involved in Catherine's case hurt the reputations of all truck drivers, most of whom are honest and hardworking people trying to provide for their families.

* * * * *

The purpose of this book is to give you some insights and perspective on what to expect following a truck crash. It wasn't written for folks in the trucking industry or for other lawyers; it was written specifically for you—our clients—to give you an understanding of the litigation process.

CHAPTER 1

WHAT MAKES
TRUCKING CASES DIFFERENT?

In your typical car crash, one or more negligent drivers failed to follow the rules of the road. Every vehicle driver should know and understand the rules of the road; we learn them as teenagers in Driver's Ed. Most of us personally follow the rules of the road every time we get into our cars.

Truck drivers also have to follow the rules of the road: yield to oncoming traffic before making a left-hand turn, follow traffic controls devices, ensure you can safely change lanes before doing so, etc. However, truck drivers and truck companies have A TON of other rules and regulations that they have to follow that you and I don't. Why? One, because these truck drivers are driving vehicles that weigh more than 20 times your average sedan. Two, because these truck drivers often spend thousands of hours driving hundreds of thousands of miles in these massive trucks every year.

Just like any specialized work, it is essential that your trucking attorney spends much of his or her time studying these regulations and understanding them. You wouldn't ask a dermatologist to treat your torn ACL because that's not his area of focus or expertise. Likewise, you shouldn't ask an attorney to handle your trucking case unless that attorney handles those types of cases every day.

HOW ARE TRUCKING CASES DIFFERENT FROM AUTO CRASH CASES?

TRUCKING CASES ARE VIGOROUSLY DEFENDED BY POWERFUL COMPANIES AND THEIR INSURERS.

When most of our clients come into our office after being injured in an automobile or truck crash, it's the first time they have been in that position. They aren't familiar with dealing with insurance companies; they're not familiar with the civil justice system; and they don't know what their rights and responsibilities are following the crash. And, why would they? Our clients typically never expect to be a victim of a crash.

Meanwhile, trucking companies and their insurers handle serious injury cases every single day. Within hours, if not minutes, of a serious trucking crash, insurance companies dispatch claims personnel to the scene to investigate the crash. Unlike crash investigations by law enforcement, these insurance company claims investigators do not aim to learn the "who, what, when, where, and whys" of the crash. Instead, they conduct their investigation with a singular focus – limit the trucking company's liability. In layman's terms, they aim to keep as much money as possible in their coffers and out of the hands of injured victims.

The unfortunate reality is that most trucking crash victims start off behind the eight ball. A good trucking insurance company has likely begun its defense of their case before the injured victim emerges from surgery. We cannot stress enough the importance of hiring a trucking attorney as soon as possible following a crash to level the fact-gathering playing field.

After the initial investigation, trucking companies and their insurers defend these cases by any means necessary. In our firm's twenty plus years, we have seen it all. From refusing to turn over company safety manuals to destroying all telephone call recordings from the company's recorded dispatch line, these companies will sometimes stop at nothing to protect their number one – the bottom line.

TRUCKING CASES TYPICALLY INVOLVE SERIOUS OR CATASTROPHIC INJURIES

All commercial motor vehicles (CMVs) have at least two things in common; they are big and they are dangerous. Whether it's an 80,000 pound semi-tractor trailer or a 50-seat charter bus, CMVs deliver a massive force when they are involved in a crash. Your everyday sedan or SUV simply isn't designed to sustain that kind of impact. Neither are human bodies. As a result, crashes involving CMVs often result in serious or catastrophic injuries.

Cases that involve significant injuries require a whole different level of expertise than a small injury case for a variety of reasons. One, the stakes are much higher. Injuries like sprains and strains often resolve on their own, without the need for specialized medical treatment. Catastrophic injuries like multiple broken bones, extensive nerve damage, and brain injuries may not resolve on their own. It's critical that victims with devastating injuries obtain **all** of the medical treatment that they require. For that reason, it's critical that you, your doctors and your attorneys have a full and complete understanding of the extent of your injuries before resolution of the case is even considered. One of the worst things that a crash victim can do is settle a lawsuit or claim for short money before understanding the complete nature of the injury. For those victims, there's no going back to the trucking insurance company years later when you have exhausted conservative treatment and your doctors recommend surgery. You only get ONE chance to recover from the insurance company.

A second difference between catastrophic cases and smaller impact cases is that most jurors have not personally experienced catastrophic injuries. A juror sitting in the jury box during a soft tissue trial likely has some understanding and personal experience with a muscle strain similar to the one experienced by the plaintiff (though the juror may be wondering why he has to take time away from his family and work for a muscle strain). On the other hand, an average juror has not experienced a devastating and debilitating injury like a tibial plateau fracture.

When you have a complicated injury, it is essential that a jury is able to step into your shoes and appreciate what you've been through. A good attorney will hire the best experts in the country to teach jurors about how this injury has affected your life since the crash, and how it will affect your life in the future. A good attorney will also make your experience palpable by using visual evidence like photographs, videos, medical devices, as well as oral evidence like the testimony of your family members that see you every day. If an attorney doesn't handle catastrophic injury cases day in and day out, he or she may not understand why it's important for juries to live through your experience or how to allow them to do it.

TRUCKING CASES REQUIRE PARTICULARIZED KNOWLEDGE OF THE TRUCKING INDUSTRY

When you have a complicated injury, *IT IS ESSENTIAL* that a jury is able to step into your shoes and appreciate what you've been through.

Today, the commercial trucking industry represents one of the largest industries in the country – and it's growing. With the rise of Amazon and other online retailers, the trucking industry simply can't find enough drivers to fulfill the staggering demand. The reality is, people aren't going to department stores or malls as much they did in the past. Instead, they're buying their products and gifts (and groceries!) from their computers and are having those goods delivered – by trucks - right to their homes.

This increased truck traffic means increased exposure of these massive vehicles to the motoring public. Make no mistake, operating trucks and other large commercial vehicles has always been dangerous business; the increased truck traffic only amplifies it. The federal government realized the potential dangers of interstate trucking as early as 1936, when they issued the first set of federal trucking safety rules. Although the federal rules have gone through several iterations over the last eighty years, the goal of these regulations has always been the same: reduce the number of injuries and deaths caused by truck-related crashes.

Every interstate trucking company must obtain "operating authority" from the U.S. Department of Transportation

(USDOT). Because trucking operations are dangerous business, the federal government makes each company certify that they have systems and procedures in place to ensure that they follow the safety rules set forth by the USDOT. Essentially, it's a promise. In exchange for this promise, the federal government allows them to earn revenue as interstate truck operators.

The current version of the federal safety rules that trucking companies must follow are called the Federal Motor Carrier Safety Regulations (FMCSRs). These regulations outline the requirements for who can operate trucks, minimum insurance coverage, driver vetting practices, drug and alcohol testing, hours of service limitations, vehicle equipment maintenance, and many other requirements.

APPLICATION FOR MOTOR PROPERTY CARRIER AND BROKER AUTHORITY - OP-1 (cont.)

SECTION IV
 	
Safety Certification (Motor Carrier Applicants Only)
	APPLICANTS SUBJECT TO FEDERAL MOTOR CARRIER SAFETY REGULATIONS - If you will operate vehicles of more than 10,000 pounds GVWR and are, thus, subject to pertinent portions of the U.S. DOT's Federal Motor Carrier Safety Regulations at 49 CFR, Chapter 3, Subchapter B (Parts 350-399), you must certify as follows:
	
	Applicant has access to and is familiar with all applicable U.S. DOT regulations relating to the safe operation of commercial vehicles and the safe transportation of hazardous materials and it will comply with these regulations. In so certifying, applicant is verifying that, at a minimum, it:
	(1) Has in place a system and an individual responsible for ensuring overall compliance with Federal Motor Carrier Safety Regulations;
	(2) Can produce a copy of the Federal Motor Carrier Safety Regulations and the Hazardous Materials Transportation Regulations;
	(3) Has in place a driver safety training/orientation program;
	(4) Has prepared and maintains an accident register (49 CFR 390.15);
	(5) Is familiar with DOT regulations governing driver qualifications and has in place a system for overseeing driver qualification requirements (49 CFR Part 391);
	(6) Has in place policies and procedures consistent with DOT regulations governing driving and operational safety of motor vehicles, including drivers' hours of service and vehicle inspection, repair, and maintenance (49 CFR Parts 392, 395 and 396);
	(7) Is familiar with and will have in place on the appropriate effective date, a system for complying with U.S. DOT regulations governing alcohol and controlled substances testing requirements (49 CFR 382 and 49 CFR Part 40).
	
	    [X] Yes
	
	EXEMPT APPLICANTS - If you will operate only small vehicles (GVWR under 10,000 pounds) and will not transport hazardous materials, you are exempt from Federal Motor Carrier Safety Regulations, and must certify as follows:
	Applicant is familiar with and will observe general operational safety guidelines, as well as any applicable State and local laws and requirements relating to the safe operation of commercial motor vehicles and the safe transportation of hazardous materials.
	
	    [X] Not Applicable

The FMCSRs represent the bare minimum standards that trucking companies must meet. In addition to these minimum rules, trucking companies must also follow what's known as "industry standards." For example, the FMCSRs do not provide specifics on what should be provided in driver safety training programs. Most trucking companies in the industry, recognizing the importance of a thorough training program, require its drivers to undergo extensive behind-the-wheel training, classroom learning and annual road tests as part of their program. A trial court is likely to find that a trucking company is obligated to follow that industry standard, even though it's not expressly identified in the FMCSRs.

Extensive knowledge of both the FMCSRs and the industry standards governing the commercial trucking industry are critical in maximizing the recovery for truck crash victims. Only by understanding every aspect of these standards can an attorney identify whether a defendant trucking company was playing by the rules.

TRUCKING CASES REQUIRE A ROBUST INVESTIGATION OF THE TRUCKING COMPANY OPERATIONS

In most automobile crash cases, the bad driver is a private citizen driving his or her own vehicle for personal use. In those cases, the crash usually happens because of a moment of neglect from one of the drivers – changing a radio station, reading a text message, failing to anticipate, or just not giving full attention to the road. Accordingly, the investigation centers on the moment of time immediately before impact.

In every trucking case, the drivers' actions immediately before a crash are obviously important and warrant a thorough investigation to determine how the crash happened. In our experience, however, we have found that the *real* cause of a crash usually occurred long before either driver got into their vehicle. In some cases, the company doesn't bother to screen the driver to determine if that driver had a terrible track record of dangerous driving. In other cases, the company hires a woefully inexperienced driver and then decides that it's too expensive to provide the necessary safety training. In all of those cases, the truck driver that caused the crash (and the victim's serious injuries) should never have been behind the wheel in the first place.

In order to figure out whether these trucking companies did all of the things they are required to do, you must obtain **all** of the relevant documents from the company. I promise you, it will be a dog fight. The only thing trucking companies and their insurers hate more than paying out big money to injured victims is handing over their "safety manuals" and "training material." Why? Because almost none of these companies follow all of the rules that they themselves set. The trucking companies' own documents bear that out time and time again. Here's an example from one of our own cases:

---

(7) Please state any thoughts that you feel are relevant to the incident, including any extenuating circumstances. (Please use the back of this form if necessary)
personally and individually I explained drivers the
rules for loading and unloading cargo- to avoid any problem. Each truck has chock inside
did not follow the rules.

Understandably, the injury to the victim represents the most important part of any truck crash case. If there's no injury, there's no recovery. The next biggest part of any trucking case may well be the conduct of the trucking company in the days, weeks, months, or even years prior to this crash. Jurors don't like corporations that don't play by the rules and they don't like companies that put the bottom line ahead of the safety of others. An exhaustive investigation of the trucking company, its documents and its own procedures should reveal whether the company could have prevented your crash long before it happened.

* * * * *

As we mentioned at the beginning of the chapter, you need an attorney that understands all of the obvious and subtle differences between a typical motor vehicle crash case and a trucking case. When we investigate a trucking case, we make sure that we turn over every single stone in trying to learn the what and the why of how each crash occurred. Given the massive impact that these crashes have on our clients lives, the stakes are too high to take half measures in investigating these cases.

CHAPTER 2

WHAT DO I DO AFTER A TRUCKING CRASH?

Under Illinois law, an individual injured due to the negligence of others typically has two years from the date of injury to file a lawsuit against the negligent party.[2] This fact doesn't mean that you should wait nearly two years before starting to pursue your case. For the reasons outlined below, it is <u>critical</u> that you speak with an attorney as soon as you are able. Trust me when I say that the trucking company's insurance carrier has already begun its investigation.

Too many times we have had prospective clients come into our office asking us to file their case right before the statute of limitations expires. Sometimes the impending statute is

---

2   This time limit, known as the "statute of limitations," can vary greatly depending on the nature of the case and the defendant being sued. For example, when suing a government entity, you may have far less than two years to file your suit. Because of these time limit variations, it is essential to talk with a lawyer as soon as possible.

beyond the control of the individual – for example, they previously hired an inexperienced attorney that failed to investigate or promptly file the case. Other times, however, these prospective clients did not understand the level of required urgency in investigating and prosecuting trucking cases. If you take one thing away from reading this book, let it be this: If you're involved in a serious truck-related accident, talk to a trucking attorney as soon as possible so that together you can start building your case for trial.

Since the vast majority of our clients have no experience with lawsuits, we've put together this chapter to give you some pointers on what to do and what *not* to do in the days, weeks, and months following a serious trucking crash.

I WAS INJURED IN A TRUCK CRASH – NOW WHAT?

ENGAGE AN ATTORNEY AS EARLY AS POSSIBLE

As we discussed in the last chapter, the trucking company's insurer began its investigation of your crash within hours of the crash. The immediate response from the insurance company almost always gives them a head start on the gathering of facts. The shorter the time gap from when the insurance company begins its investigation and someone on your behalf begins their investigation, the better it is for your case.

AVOID TALKING TO INSURANCE COMPANIES

When an insurance company calls you, refer them to your attorney immediately. Insurance adjusters can be ruthless. Oftentimes, they will attempt to ask you information about the crash or your medical treatment. Your situation is your business! Not the business of the negligent trucking company. They are not asking for this information because they're trying to help you. Rather, they're looking for any piece of information that will limit the amount of money that their company has to pay you. Adjusters have been known to advise injured victims against hiring an attorney or recommend that you sign a release absolving them.

FOCUS ON YOUR PHYSICAL, MENTAL, AND EMOTIONAL RECOVERY

When you have been injured in a crash, the last thing on your mind should be dealing with insurance companies and bill collectors. Every time we meet with a new client, we ask them to delegate the stress and anxiety inherent in litigation to us. Let us shoulder the burdens of litigation; we do it every day. By not allowing yourself to get bogged down with the minutiae of a lawsuit, an injured victim can focus on what's most important – getting your health back.

Whenever someone or something threatens to shift your focus from your recovery to "How am I going to pay for this?" or "Is this document important?", let your attorney know. You can help make your attorney's job easier by simply saving documents that come in and forwarding them to the law office.

BEGIN TO COLLECT ITEMS FOR TRIAL

At the end of your trucking case, you (and your lawyers) will have an opportunity to tell your story to twelve jurors. These jurors are the finders of fact that will determine whether you're entitled to compensation as a result of the crash, as well as determine the value of your case. These twelve people aren't professional jurors; they're teachers, nurses, construction workers. They absorb information in different ways. A particular piece of evidence may be extremely compelling to one witness and relatively unimportant to another. It's important that your attorneys understand how to communicate with each member of the jury panel.

In our experience, there is one unequivocal truth in every jury trial – the most effective trial evidence is visual. Across the board, jurors have a better understanding of how your injury has affected your life if you're able to **show** the jury the effect, rather than **tell** them the effect. It's one thing to tell a jury that you went to dozens of physical therapy sessions to rehabilitate your injuries. It's another thing entirely to show them a video of you in physical therapy, wearing a gait belt, using a walker and struggling to go even a few feet without needing to take a break.

From the moment after a crash occurs, you and your family should be collecting items that your attorney can use at trial to show the jury your experience. Some of these essential visual items include braces, casts, surgical hardware, crutches, walkers, wheelchairs, the clothes you wore on the day of the crash. In addition to collecting the tangible items, it is also important to document your experience with photographs and videos. Some of our clients hesitate when we ask them to document their recovery, and it's completely understandable. Recovery from catastrophic injuries is ugly. People don't typically like to showcase their

In our experience, there is one unequivocal truth in every jury trial – the most effective trial evidence is visual.

lives at their most vulnerable moments. We get it; it can be uncomfortable. That said, it's critical that a jury understands the truth about what you've been through – the good, the bad and the ugly.

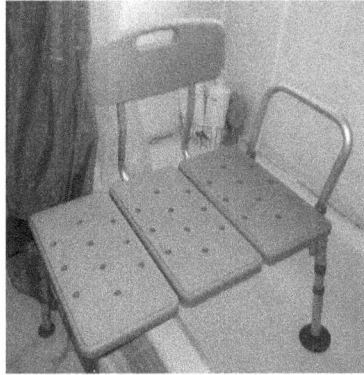

BE SMART ABOUT SOCIAL MEDIA

Defense lawyers constantly monitor social media accounts of injured plaintiffs. If you claim that you're unable to work because of your shoulder injury, you shouldn't be posting videos from your hang-gliding vacation on Facebook. That's not to say you need to lock yourself in your home until your case is over. Just recognize that anything that you put out on social media is being viewed by insurance companies and defense lawyers. If what you wouldn't want a potential juror to see or read the post you're about to make, don't post it. Our advice: Take a break from social media and concentrate on getting better.

COLLECT MEDICAL RECORDS AND BILLS FOR YOUR ATTORNEY

Any time you get a bill from a provider or a collection agency, you should immediately forward it to your attorney.

First, it's important that your attorney knows each and every provider that has treated you for your injuries. This can be more complicated than it seems. Even if you only treated at one physical locations, there could be separate entities and billing departments for each doctor that treated you. In order to make sure that you recover **all** of your medical bills, it's important that you help your attorney by sending him these bills. Sometimes our clients want to keep the bills for their own personal file. At our firm, we scan in any bill we receive and make the originals available for the client if he or she wants to keep them for their own records.

Second, your attorney can help shoulder the stress of your medical treatment by calling up providers and bill collectors to let them know your case is in litigation. Typically, we will ask them to bill your health insurer (it's usually in the provider's best interest to do so anyway). Either way, we'll inform them that you are represented, and have them direct all calls to us so that you're not dealing with constant calls from creditors.

MEMORIALIZE YOUR EXPERIENCES IN A MEMO TO YOUR ATTORNEY

All communication between you and us is confidential and protected by attorney-client privilege. As such, we ask most of our clients to write us a memo documenting the injury since the date of the crash. For example, you should be noting days when you have physical therapy, particularly painful or difficult activities, headaches, stresses, difficulty sleeping, and other noteworthy ways that your injury complicates your life. This memo helps us understand exactly what you've been going through so that we can adequately explain it to a jury. It also helps you identify and remember all of the different ways that the injury has affected your daily life.

Make sure that you title the memo "To My Attorney" so that it is clear that this memo is protected.

CHECK YOUR INSURANCE POLICY FOR MEDICAL PAYMENT COVERAGE

Many personal automobile insurance policies have something called medical payment coverage ("MedPay"). If you have MedPay coverage, your own insurance company will pay you for medical bills incurred up to the limits of your coverage. Say you have $3,500 worth of hospital bills from the day of the crash and a $5,000 limit for MedPay coverage. You can submit those bills to your insurer who then should write you a check for $3,500. If you have retained an attorney, he should be able to recover your MedPay for you.

MedPay coverage can be a lifesaver for clients when their medical bills from the crash quickly start to add up. It's important to note that when your insurance company pays you MedPay, it is essentially a loan. At the end of the case, if you recover from the trucking company's insurer, your insurance company will want back a portion of what they paid you in MedPay through a process called subrogation. An experienced injury attorney will be able to explain in detail this process to you should you have questions about it.

* * * * *

If you follow the above rules, your case will run more smoothly, and you can rest easy knowing that you have provided all of the tools necessary for a capable trucking attorneys to maximize your recovery. If you are ever curious about any part of the litigation process or how certain social media post (e.g., of your family's rock-climbing trip) may impact your case, do not hesitate to ask your attorneys any questions.

CHAPTER 3

IS MY CASE EVEN A TRUCKING CASE?

HOW DO I KNOW IF I NEED A LAWYER WHO SPECIALIZES IN TRUCKING?

When a fatigued semi-trailer driver falls asleep and barrels through stopped traffic on a highway, it's obvious to everyone that the case would be considered a "trucking case." However, there are many situations where it might not be so obvious. In this chapter, we discuss a variety of cases that require an attorney with specialized knowledge of the trucking and commercial transportation industry.

"COMMERCIAL MOTOR VEHICLES"

A "commercial motor vehicle" (CMV) is a term of art within the transportation industry and legal community. CMV operators have many more rules and regulations that they must follow than the everyday driver. Why? Because CMVs spend more time on the road and because their size makes them much more dangerous than a sedan.

Many types of vehicles you might not expect qualify as CMVs. In Catherine's case, she was hit by a roadside service truck. The company had retrofitted an old ambulance by removing the large box trailer and installing a smaller service repair trailer. Essentially, the vehicle looked like a slightly larger Ford F-350 – a vehicle that any licensed driver can lawfully drive on public roads. The roadside service company itself failed to recognize that the modified vehicle qualified as a CMV and was subject to countless additional regulations.

In another recent case, the defendant driver was driving his pickup truck to a truck pulling event (motorsport contest in which a heavily modified pickup truck pulls weighted sleds down a track) with his friends. His pickup truck was trailing a large trailer carrying the souped-up truck pull pickup truck. Driving such a long and heavy vehicle requires special training and skill, which is why that combination truck and trailer qualified as a CMV. Again, the defendant driver failed to follow the rules; he didn't possess the driver's license certification required to drive that vehicle. Predictably, the driver dangerously attempted to make a left hand turn from a right hand lane that ended up permanently injuring our client.

When you or someone close to you is involved in a vehicle crash, it is essential to have attorneys that can identify CMVs even when the company operating the vehicle cannot.

UNDERSTANDING THE PARTIES AND INSURANCE COVERAGE IN COMMERCIAL TRANSPORTATION CASES

In order to maximize your recovery, your trucking attorney needs to understand the many moving parts involved every time a trucking company carries freight. Many years ago, the trucking industry was fairly simple. The milk companies manufactured the milk, bottled the milk, loaded the milk into their own truck, and employed their own drivers to deliver the milk to their customers.

Nowadays, the commercial transportation industry looks more like a complex labyrinth of manufacturers, large shippers, logistics brokers, and owner-operator trucking companies. A single truck carrying goods from Los Angeles to Chicago may involve ten or more different entities. Each one of those entities earns money as a result of the freight shipment and each entity has certain responsibilities to ensure that the goods are shipped efficiently, cost-effectively, and safely.

Many small mom-and-pop trucking companies carry only the minimum insurance coverage required by law. In cases involving serious injuries or death, the minimum insurance coverage does not come close to compensating you adequately. In order to recover fair compensation, you will need an experienced trucking attorney who understands all of the machinations of the industry and the insurance covering each shipment.

* * * * *

A couple of years ago, we had a truck driver client, John, who was injured when he fell off the back of his truck attempting to unload a large commercial sink from the back of his truck. When he pulled on the wooden crate encasing the sink, the wooden slat snapped, and John's momentum caused him to fall out of the back of the truck and onto the asphalt below. He suffered catastrophic injuries to his leg.

Obviously, we knew that the people that manufactured the crate were negligent. They used a poor design and shoddy materials. Our past experience, however, led us to other parties who contributed to John's injury.

After reviewing all of the contracts and investigative reports, we learned that the construction company supervising the delivery site was responsible for unloading the crate and sink. Making matters worse, they parked a dumpster right in front of the loading dock at the worksite, making it inaccessible to John and other delivery drivers. Had John been able to park his truck at the loading dock, he likely would have only fallen four or five inches and sustained nothing worse than a rolled ankle. Instead, he fell almost four feet directly onto his leg.

We also discovered that the crate manufacturer had hired a broker company to facilitate the delivery of the crate. In its contract and federal filings, the broker promises to manage all aspects of the shipping process through the entire life cycle of a shipment. This meant that the broker promised to make sure that the delivery and unloading of this crate went smoothly.

In that case, the broker didn't keep their promise. They never informed the construction company when the delivery was arriving and accordingly, the dumpster could not be moved from the dock and the inoperable forklift's battery could not be replaced in a timely manner. If the construction company had known the timing of the sink's arrival, it could have taken steps to ensure that the equipment necessary for safe unloading was available and ready for use.

By the time we were ready to pick our jury at trial, all three parties contributed to John's settlement. Understanding the responsibilities of all the entities involved in that delivery allowed us to maximize John's recovery and ensure that he was fairly and completely compensated for his permanent injuries.

CHAPTER 4

WHAT CAN I RECOVER IN MY TRUCKING CRASH CASE?

INTRODUCTION

A couple of years ago our client, Alex, was a thirty-year-old forklift operator working at a warehouse in Chicago. His job included unloading palletized freight off of tractor-trailers. For ten years, Alex had been working hard at this job every day, providing for himself. At nights, Alex was moonlighting as a commercial glassworker known as a glazier. His dad and cousins had worked for years as glaziers in one of the local unions. Alex wanted to join the family business and become a journeyman glazier. A union glazier position represented a huge financial opportunity for Alex.

Alex had taken and passed the test to become a union member, he had gone down to the union hall to find a list of union contractors that were looking for apprentices, he called dozens of those contractors and ultimately secured several interviews. And then his life changed forever.

One summer day, Alex received paperwork from a truck driver indicating that the truck was secured to the loading dock and that it was safe for Alex to drive his forklift onto the trailer and begin unloading. One problem – the truck driver hadn't actually secured his truck to the dock. When Alex drove his forklift onto the trailer, the unsecured trailer rolled away from the dock and the 9,000-pound forklift crashed to the ground with Alex inside.

In the fall, Alex sustained permanent spinal injuries that left him unable to return to work as forklift driver, much less handle the physical rigors of a union glazier. His injuries robbed him of a career. But Alex wasn't a complainer or a quitter; he went back to work in a light duty role within two weeks of his injury.

Because his company agreed to keep his wage rates the same, Alex had only missed out on a couple weeks of lost wages. The defendant insurance company and their attorneys viewed it as a case of almost zero lost earnings. But what about his lost career as a glazier?

We hired one of the best economic experts in the country to calculate what Alex's lost earning capacity would be over his entire working life as a result of his injuries. That economist concluded that Alex's lost career as a journeyman union member cost him well over a million dollars over the course of his work life. All of a sudden, the value of Alex's case skyrocketed in the eyes of the insurance company defending it.

At our firm, we are constantly thinking of ways to maximize our client's recovery – to make sure that they are fairly compensated for *all* of their losses. By thinking big and outside-the-box, we were able to provide Alex and his family with lifelong financial security.

WHAT CAN I RECOVER IN MY TRUCKING CRASH CASE?

At Shannon Law Group, our job is simple. We help people get back what was taken from them. We tell many of our clients that we are glorified debt collectors. Someone has been broken because of the negligence of a truck driver or systemic failures of a trucking company. We have to try and fix that injured person with money. Why do we fix them with money? Because we can't undo the often-catastrophic injuries in someone's body. Under the civil justice system, we use money to attempt to make an injured victim whole again. It's not a perfect system, but it's the best that we have.

An injured truck crash victim can recover for any injuries that she sustained in the crash. Compensable injuries can include completely traumatic injuries like broken bones. They can include aggravation or worsening of pre-existing injuries like arthritis. Compensable injuries can also include something called "increased risk of harm." Say, for example, a truck hits you and as a result, you become much more susceptible to a certain condition in the future. A jury may decide that a trucking company should pay for that increased vulnerability.

At Shannon Law Group, our job is simple. We help people get back what was taken from them. We tell many of our clients that we are glorified debt collectors.

ECONOMIC DAMAGES

MEDICAL BILLS

Economic Damages are what we call "easy to calculate" damages. The most obvious portion of economic damages is an injured victim's medical bills. Many new clients mistakenly believe that the bad driver's insurance company will pay their medical bills as they come in. Unfortunately, it doesn't work like that. Typically, a defendant's insurance company won't pay anything for your medical bills until the very end of the case because a court has ordered them to pay the bills or because you have settled the case.

During the pendency of your case, it's important to ask your medical providers to bill your health insurer directly. After all, you pay health insurance premiums every month for this exact reason. Sometimes healthcare providers will try to bill you personally instead of doing what they should do and bill your health insurance. Why? Some providers think that they can recover more from you (and your settlement or judgment proceeds) than the rate at which your health insurer agrees to pay the bill.

In many of our cases, especially truck crash cases with serious injuries, our clients are not done with their medical treatment at the time the case resolves. What happens if you need a surgery or more therapy at the time the case is wrapping up? Don't panic – it's a situation that arises every day. If you require future medical treatment, the defendant and their insurance company are still on the hook. How? Because you're entitled to recover compensation for *all* medical bills that you have to incur because of the crash—including those reasonably likely to occur in the future. To do this, one of your treating doctors or an expert doctor hired will project for the jury what treatment you are likely to need going forward and how much that treatment will cost.

Here's a sample verdict form that shows the different types of damages to which you may be entitled.

WHAT EACH DAMAGES ELEMENT MEANS

LOST WAGES

In addition to paying for the medical bills you incurred, the defendant trucking company will also have to compensate you for any lost wages you experienced. That includes time missed from work while in the hospital or before your doctor cleared you to return to work. It also includes any time missed for surgeries, therapy and doctor's visits.

LOSS OF EARNING CAPACITY

Sometimes our clients have permanent injuries that will prevent them from ever going back to their old job. If the only job that they can find (that they're physically capable of doing) earns less money than their previous job, they can recover for that difference. To do so, your trucking attorney will sometimes hire an economist to calculate that difference for the rest of your working life.

LOSS OF HOUSEHOLD SERVICES

A jury may also find that you are entitled to damages for the loss of household services that you have experienced and will experience in the future as a result of your injuries. Household services include things like cooking, cleaning, mowing the lawn and doing your laundry. Say, for example, you were able to do all of those things before the crash. After the crash, you can only do half of those things in the same amount of time. An economist may be called to explain to the jury the value of the services that you can no longer complete in an average day.

PROPERTY DAMAGE

Most truck crashes involve massive damage to the vehicles involved. If your vehicle is damaged or totaled in a crash, you can recover the amount of damage or value of the vehicle from the defendant trucking company. Where an injured victim has collision coverage on his or her own automobile insurance coverage, the insurance company may write you a check for the damage. In that case, the company will pursue recovery of the check they paid you from the truck insurer directly through a process called subrogation. Check out the FAQs chapter for more insight on recovering for the damage to your vehicle.

NON-ECONOMIC DAMAGES

After a catastrophic injury, the greatest losses are often what we call non-economic damages. Non-economic damages seek to rectify an injured victim's loss of joy in living their daily life. Folks with serious injuries experience pain doing activities that most of us take for granted everyday–putting on a sweater, walking the dog, playing soccer with your kids, or planting perennials in your garden. Many times, these injuries either prevent injured victims from participating in favorite hobbies altogether or severely limits their ability to enjoy activities that they used to love.

Unlike economic damages, non-economic damages are not easily calculable. Non-economic damages are subjectively determined by the jury. Different juries in different counties may award completely different non-economics damages for the same set of facts. Because the jury instructions do not provide jurors with much guidance in reaching an appropriate award figure for non-economic damages, it can be difficult for juries to assign a monetary value to these losses. Likewise, it is extremely difficult to predict what any given jury would award for non-economic damages in your case.

PAIN AND SUFFERING

Though commonly referred to as one collective component of damages, pain and suffering has two distinct elements: the physical pain and the mental suffering caused by the injuries. The physical pain includes the immediate pain after the crash, the pain and discomfort experienced since the day of the crash, and the adverse physical effects that the victim is likely suffer in the future as a result of the injuries.

Mental suffering is the derivative negative emotional effects caused by your injury. It includes things like mental anguish, emotional distress, depression, hopelessness, fear, embarrassment, anxiety, and trouble sleeping, among others. Like the physical pain element, mental suffering also accounts for both past and future suffering.

In most serious injury cases, the pain and suffering component is one of the largest components of damages. Why? Because in many truck crash cases, the injuries victims sustain are permanent – which means that they will live with pain and discomfort every single day. If it's a severe leg injury, that means pain with every step. If it's a significant shoulder injury, it could mean pain every time you carry in groceries or unload the dishwasher.

But, how do you prove pain and suffering? You and your attorney have to be able to educate the jury about the impact your injuries have had on your daily life. To do that, you must make it visual for a jury – show, don't merely tell. Photographs and videos illustrating your rehabilitation help a jury put themselves in your shoes. We typically ask our clients to save braces, casts, crutches, walkers and other medical devices that they had to use during their recovery. We show juries all of it – even if it's ugly. It's essential to helping them understand just how difficult this crash has made your life.

You will have an opportunity to talk to the jury about your injuries during your direct examination. In addition, your attorney may decide to call your family members or friends to testify about how you've been affected. Oftentimes, the best person to explain your pain and suffering to a jury is not the injured victim. Instead, it's usually someone close to the injured person, who sees you every day and can describe to the jury, from an outside perspective, the painful impact your injury has had on your life.

If properly educated about the extent of your expected future pain,, a jury may award damages for the hundreds or thousands of painful moments you can expect to experience over the remainder of your life.

LOSS OF A NORMAL LIFE

In Illinois, courts allow juries to award damages for "loss of a normal life." The jury instructions define loss of a normal life as "the temporary or permanent diminished ability to enjoy life. This includes a person's inability to pursue the pleasurable aspects of life." So, what does that entail?

For example, after certain injuries, people who previously enjoyed an active lifestyle of hiking, playing basketball with their kids, and taking long walks with the dog are unable to continue those hobbies pain-free, if they're able to do them at all. These are the hobbies that are clients live for. As we tell juries all the time, we don't live our lives to go to work and pay our medical bills; we live for the weekends and nights spent with our family and friends.

If an injury alters a client's life such that they are unable to continue participating in some of their passions, that is a huge loss for that client. Jurors understand this. Any juror in a case can picture eliminating one of their favorite pastimes and understand how the alteration can make it harder for a plaintiff to enjoy his or her life.

Like pain and suffering, a properly educated jury may award loss of a normal life for the many instances of an altered life that you may experience as a result of your injuries.

DISFIGUREMENT

Trucking crash injuries will often leave victims with permanent scarring or disfigurement. This may include burns, surgical scars, or bone / joint deformities. Like the other categories of damages, a jury may award disfigurement damages for both past and future disfigurement. If you have scarring or other disfigurement, it is essential that the disfigurement is well-documented with photographs and videos. If you are going to ask a jury for compensation for a disfigurement, you will need to be able to clearly show them the disfigurement you've suffered and how it has affected your life.

PUNITIVE DAMAGES

Punitive Damages are damages awarded by a jury that are intended to punish the defendants for their egregious conduct and deter other trucking companies from behaving that way in the future. Currently, there is no cap on punitive damages in Illinois, but the amount awarded will depend on whether a jury believes the trucking company's conduct to be shocking or appalling.

In a recent commercial transportation trial, the jury awarded our client a half million dollars in punitive damages because of the complete lack of safety systems employed by the company. That company, like many we've run into over the years, made absolutely ZERO effort to screen its drivers or train them. In fact, our expert testified that the company's driver vetting procedures (or lack thereof) were the worst he's ever seen in his thirty-five years in the industry.

CHAPTER 5

HOW CAN A TRUCKING ATTORNEY HELP ME?

An obvious first question for someone who has just been involved in any sort of vehicle crash is, "Do I need an attorney?" The short answer is: "It depends." If you're involved in a fender bender collision with no injuries and little or no property damage, you very well may be able to adequately handle the case on your own. At Shannon Law Group, we will not hesitate in telling someone who comes into our office that they would be able to net more money in their pocket by prosecuting their property damage case versus hiring an attorney to do it for them. We even have guidelines that we give to those individuals that help Sherpa them through the insurance property claim or small claims court by themselves without the expense of hiring a lawyer.

On the other side of the injury spectrum are those individuals that suffer catastrophic injuries in a collision. In those situations, we cannot stress enough the importance of hiring a great trucking law firm as soon as possible. Simply put, a trucking company's insurer will never offer you what your case is worth. Why? Because they know that (a) you don't have the familiarity with injury litigation to appreciate the full value of your case, and (b) you don't have the resources, experience, and knowledge to maximize the value of your case like a seasoned trucking attorney would.

If you or someone you know suffers devastating injuries in a crash, recommend that they reach out to an attorney immediately. As we note in other chapters, insurance companies will stop at nothing to prevent you from seeking legal counsel – in turn, saving the insurance companies' money, all at your expense now and in the future.

Obviously, the two scenarios described above leaves a wide gap of collision situations in between. A good general rule of thumb is this: if there are injuries that required medical treatment – particularly EMT or ER treatment on the day of the crash – it's worth your time sitting down with a lawyer to discuss your options. Below, we've outlined some of the key areas in which a trucking attorney can help you after a serious crash.

DELEGATE THE STRESS OF LITIGATION TO SOMEONE ELSE

Possibly the most important service we provide to our clients involves shouldering the burden and stresses of a lawsuit for them. Without trucking lawyers providing a necessary buffer between an injured victim and insurance companies, bill collectors, and defense counsel, litigation can be an overwhelming experience for the uninitiated. I've had many clients over the years express gratitude for us because it allows them to simply collect any relevant documents or mail, send them to our office and know that we will take care of whatever needs to be done.

Delegating the stress of litigation to your attorneys allows to you place all of your energy and focus on your recovery. That's where the focus should be. No one wants to drown in court paperwork, insurance policies, and medical bills when they are attempting to adapt to their new normal.

Your attorney will also prepare you for the only two times you will be asked to tell your story – at deposition and at trial. If not properly prepared, a deposition can be an anxiety-ridden environment. The adversarial nature of the civil justice system means that the trucking company lawyers are not there to merely hear your story; they're asking you questions to find any way they can keep more money out of your hands and in the pockets of their insurance company. A good lawyer will not only have you prepared for your deposition (so you know what kinds of questions to expect), but will also protect you from any inappropriate or irrelevant questions asked by opposing counsel at your deposition.

BUILD AND IMPROVE YOUR CASE

Injured clients and their attorneys should have perfectly aligned goals: putting the most money in the client's pocket as possible. During an initial intake meeting, Joe Shannon will often tell a prospective client that the lawyers at our firm our glorified debt collectors. Someone seriously injured you and it's our job to go collect what they owe you.

In order to maximize your net recovery, you need to have a cohesive reason to tell a jury about WHY this crash happened. In almost every trucking case, the defense lawyers will attempt to make the case about the 5-10 seconds immediately before a crash. Even when a trucking company ultimately admits that their driver screwed up, the defense lawyer will attribute it to a momentary lack of attention or lapse in judgment by a driver.

In reality, the WHY of your crash occurred begins long before the impact of the crash. It starts with the hiring of the driver and the development of the company's driver training programs. In some cases, it goes as far back as the inception of the defendant trucking company – when they had to file certifications to the federal government promising that they would operate a safe trucking company.

In building your liability case against a trucking company, your attorney needs to learn and understand all of the trucking company's procedures involving driver hiring, training and supervision. Was the company playing by the rules? Did the company ever put the bottom line ahead of safety? Oftentimes, a thorough investigation reveals that the trucking company cut safety corners to save a few bucks. Hiring a great trucking safety expert to peel back the onion of a trucking operation and determine whether it was doing things the right way will garner the most favorable result possible.

A great trucking attorney will also present your case to a jury in a way that is compelling, visual and easy to understand. Jurors want to SEE how your injuries have impacted your life, not just hear about it. Your attorneys should use photographs, videos, animations, and timelines, along with expert doctor testimony, to describe to a jury how your life has been affected since the crash and how it will likely be affected in the future. If a jury can FEEL the harms that you've suffered, they will allow a fair verdict amount.

GUIDE YOU THROUGH THE LAWSUIT

A good attorney will act as your Sherpa through the often complex world of litigation. Your attorney should advise you on how to best preserve your rights and your claims before and throughout the litigation process, including when and with whom you can disclose facts about your case.

Your attorney should also help to set reasonable expectations for your case. In 99% of our cases, our clients have zero understanding of the reasonable value of the case. Your attorneys can often help advise you on the range of recovery for similarly situated individuals in your jurisdiction. Obviously, these figures would be ranges based on our experience. It is impossible to pinpoint an exact value of a case when you will be asking twelve strangers in a jury box to come to a unanimous decision on the value.

If a jury can FEEL the harms that you've suffered, they will allow a fair verdict amount.

At Shannon Law Group, our job is to tell you the truth about your case. If there's good news, we will tell you. If there's bad news, we will deliver that to you as well. We are not in the business of sugarcoating or glossing over difficult aspects of your case.

Finally, a great attorney will counsel you on all the benefits available to you, including insurance, disability or unemployment benefits.

PROTECT YOUR RECOVERY

Our job does not end when we obtain a favorable verdict or settlement for our clients. We strive to be the attorneys you call for the rest of your life with any legal problem you have. In furthering that mission, we make sure we advise you on the best way to protect any recovery you achieve in your case. That includes advising you on the pros and cons of structured settlements, negotiating with lien holders to resolve liens, or put you in the hands of the best professionals (financial advisers, accountants, tax attorneys) in the area depending on your specific needs.

CHAPTER 6

HOW DOES MY TRUCKING LAWSUIT WORK? A STEP-BY-STEP GUIDELINE OF LITIGATION AND WHAT TO EXPECT

Fortunately for them, the vast majority of our clients have ZERO experience with litigation and the civil justice system when they first walk in our door. For these clients, everything in the process is foreign and new. When we explain to clients how long the process may last before they ever see a dime, their jaws often hit the floor. In Cook County, it's often 2+ years from the time a complaint is filed until the date of trial. Unfortunately, the gears of justice grind slowly. To help folks understand the general process of civil litigation, we put together a litigation timeline so that clients can better understand what to expect throughout the process.

INVESTIGATION

Before an attorney can file a complaint alleging that a trucking company (or any other defendant) was negligent, he must first investigate the incident to determine whether he can successfully prosecute the case. At Shannon Law Group, we typically will not take a case unless we're willing to try that case in front of twelve jurors. Why? One, because if we don't believe in the case and don't believe completely that we can come through for our client, it makes it extremely difficult to provide the requisite level of zealous advocacy for that client.

In order to get to the point where we decide that we are willing to try a particular case, we have to conduct a thorough investigation of the underlying facts. Two, because we recognize the sacrifice that jurors make resolving disputes every day. These jurors are regular people that have families, jobs and personal lives that become disrupted when they are called to hear cases in our courts. For that reason, we won't sign up a case unless we will be able to explain to jurors at the end of the case that they're doing something important and that the case being presented to them is worth their time away from their lives.

In a typical trucking crash case, there will be a police report summarizing the police department's investigation of the crash. In Illinois, it's on a form called the Illinois Traffic Crash Report. You may be given a form at the scene known as the Illinois Motorist Report. This form doesn't contain a narrative of the events of the crash; instead, the purpose of the motorist report is merely to provide all of the drivers involved in the crash with the personal and insurance information of the other drivers. The Illinois Traffic Crash Report, while

ILLINOIS TRAFFIC CRASH REPORT

sometimes hastily investigated and carelessly summarized, usually provides a good generalized statement of how and why a crash occurred. More importantly, it provides attorneys with key information from which they can begin a more robust investigation.

First, the crash report identifies any known witnesses to the crash. Once we receive a crash report, we immediately dispatch our investigators to interview the known witnesses. These early witness statements can make or break a case. Years ago, we represented a motorcycle driver who was involved in a crash when a pickup truck and attached trailer attempted to make a left-hand turn from a right-side merge lane across several lanes of traffic. The maneuver was so unexpected and instant that our client had to lay his bike down in the highway (at 60+ mph) to avoid an even-more catastrophic crash. Because he had to react so suddenly, he didn't have a great understanding of how the crash happened.

Fortunately for his case, our investigator found a witness, an off-duty police officer, who was driving behind our client at the time of the crash. Once our investigator obtained the off-duty officer's written statement, the negligence of the truck driver was all but proven. Had we not had our investigator start his investigation the moment the case came into our office, that statement – and the case, might have been lost.

Second, the crash report identifies the location of the crash and where any vehicles have been moved. For every trucking crash case we have, we try to go to the scene as soon as we can. We are looking for any cameras that may have captured the crash; we take photographs of the roadway as the drivers would have seen it at the time of the crash; and, if possible, we talk to some of the local neighbors and business owners to see whether they have any information about the crash.

Third, we make sure to find the vehicles that were involved in the crash. Sometimes this is an easy process. If we get a call within hours or days of a crash, we can usually go to the impound lot to take photos of vehicles. Sometimes though, if we don't sign up a case until months after a crash, we have to track down the vehicle (or its parts) across state lines and oftentimes through multiple owners. The vehicles involved in the crash can provide a treasure trove of information.

One, photographs of the vehicles can paint a picture of how a crash occurred and can help explain to a jury how our client suffered such significant injuries. If the impact crushed door panels and axels, imagine what it could do to our client's spine. Two, many newer cars (and most semi-tractor trailers) have on-board computers that provide a TON of information including the speed of the vehicle prior to impact, whether the vehicle attempted to swerve before impact, or how long before impact the driver applied the brakes.

Some trucking companies now require their vehicles to be equipped with forward-facing and driver-facing dashboard cameras. For those companies, we can see exactly what the driver saw at the moments before impact AND we can see what the driver was doing during those moments. Obviously, these can be critical sources of evidence for your case.

PLEADINGS AND MOTION PRACTICE

Once an extensive investigation has been completed and your case has been determined to have merit, your attorney will file a complaint against the trucking company that hit you. Typically, the complaint will be against both the trucking company and the driver individually – though usually both entities are covered by the same insurance policy. A filed complaint then needs to be served upon all defendants (usually the trucking company and the individual driver) by a sheriff. Once the complaint is served on the defendants, the defendants have a chance to answer all of your complaint allegations and make any affirmative defenses they may have.

In some cases, the trucking company will file a motion asking the court to dismiss your complaint because of a technical defect. Courts historically are very liberal in allowing plaintiffs to amend their complaint to correct any technical defects. Your attorney will handle all of the filings and court appearances during this portion of the case. Depending on a number of different factors, this portion of the case can take as little as 1-2 months up to nearly a year.

WRITTEN DISCOVERY

The next step in the litigation process is known as written discovery. During this phase, all parties have the opportunity to ask the other side questions (interrogatories) about them and the circumstances of the case, including asking parties to identify known witnesses, past injuries, driving history, among other items. In addition, the parties will ask the other side to provide numerous documents related to the case. Defendants typically request police reports, witness statements, as well as medical records from before and after the crash. Plaintiffs typically request internal investigation documents, as well as documents related to the trucking company's vetting and training of the driver involved in the crash.

During this process, your attorney will need your assistance to promptly and accurately provide the answers and documents requested by the defendants. Historically, trucking companies never provide all of the documents requested of them right away. Thus, it can often take many months and sometimes court intervention to spur the trucking company to provide all of the documents related to the crash.

In most cases, a trucking company's own documents (or lack of documents) make the best evidence in proving that the company was negligent. The Federal Motor Carrier Safety Regulations, which govern the operations of most large trucking companies, require a number of documents to be kept in order for the company to retain its operating authority. Operating heavy tractor-trailers and other commercial motor vehicles is by nature dangerous business, and the federal government recognizes that. In exchange for allowing an interstate motor carrier to make money operating trucks, the federal government requires the company to guarantee that it will operate according to the safety rules put in place by the federal regulations.

In most cases, a trucking company's own documents (or lack of documents) make the best evidence in proving that the company was negligent.

Among the rules that trucking companies promise to follow are having in place certain minimum standards for driver quality, driver hours of service, drug and alcohol testing, vehicle condition, accident monitoring and document production. These guarantees are akin to a social contract. Authorized motor carriers have made a promise to play by the safety rules. When these companies don't follow the rules or remain willfully ignorant of their obligations, they break their promise.

Unfortunately, we have seen some abysmal trucking companies over the years that either decide they're above the safety rules or don't bother to learn the rules in the first place. On more occasions than you'd believe, trucking companies and other commercial transportation companies hire drivers without so much as checking their driving history or their criminal record – both of which are required by the regulations. Other companies claim to fulfill their driver training obligations, but don't actually have any paperwork documenting whether any training was actually provided to a particular driver. The written discovery process allows your attorney to learn what the defendant trucking company did or did not do that could have prevented your crash from ever occurring.

DEPOSITIONS

A deposition is an oral testimony taken under oath before a trial or arbitration. It is customary that depositions be taken of the parties to a lawsuit. Often depositions are also taken of witnesses who might testify at trial. Even though it often takes place in a conference room or office, and the setting is somewhat informal, it is a very important event in any lawsuit.

The questions you will be asked pertain to information relevant to your trucking crash accident case. For example, you will be asked about your medical, employment and educational background, and about the crash and your injuries. Your deposition will probably take between one and three hours. Your attorney will be there with you when you are questioned by the other attorney.

The deposition allows the lawyer on the other side to "discover" all the facts a witness may know which will assist that lawyer in preparing for the trial or arbitration of a case. It may also be the only opportunity the other lawyer has to evaluate you as a witness. The biggest rule in depositions is to tell the truth. If your case goes to trial, the defense attorney will have the transcript of your deposition testimony and will not hesitate in reading it back to you if there are any inconsistencies in your trial testimony.

Who gets deposed depends on the attorneys involved in the case. We have had cases in which the opposing counsel took the deposition of every medical doctor that treated our client – forty plus depositions. In other cases, the opposing counsel may only take the deposition of you and one or two of your treating doctors. In some cases, your spouse, family members, friends or co-workers may also be deposed so that the attorneys can learn what those witnesses know about your injuries and how they have affected your life.

Prior to your deposition, your attorney will meet with you to go over the kinds of questions that you can expect to hear at your deposition. Your attorney may even cross examine you during your preparation meeting so that you are not experiencing cross examination for the first time at your deposition. Depending on how many witnesses, treating doctors, and experts need to be deposed in a given case, the oral testimony portion of the case may be the longest lasting of the entire litigation. Doctors, especially, have difficult and busy schedules that may require scheduling their deposition months in advance.

SETTLEMENT NEGOTIATIONS

In any trucking case, there are two tracks that run through the entire litigation. On one hand, there's the litigation track (described above) that runs through the court system and is generally governed by court rules and deadlines. The litigation track ends with a trial so everything on that track focuses on trial preparation.

On the other hand, there's the settlement track which can often be a winding and seemingly aimless path. The reality in litigation is that insurance companies control the purse strings. At any time throughout the case, the insurance company can decide that they want to stop spending money defending the case and instead make a settlement offer to the injured plaintiff. Unfortunately, you and your attorneys do not control when an insurance company decides to transition a case from a trial posture to a settlement posture.

Because you and your attorneys don't control when an insurance company wants to seek resolution, it is important that your attorney prepare every case as if it's going all the way to trial. At Shannon Law Group, our motto is, "We won't file a case if we're not willing to try it." If we agree to file your case, we believe strongly in your case and want to share your story with a jury. That mentality has garnered great results for our clients in the past and we anticipate it will continue to do so in the future.

TRIAL

As you've already read in this book, the vast majority of cases do not go all the way to trial. But what is a trial anyway? A trial is you and your attorneys' opportunity to present evidence to a jury – to explain the how and why your truck crash occurred and more importantly, to explain how your injuries have affected your life since the crash. The trial also provides the defendant trucking company a chance to explain their actions. Your trial represents the last step before a jury of twelve citizens decides how much money your case is worth.

Trials tend to involve a level of uncertainty for plaintiffs and insurance company. For plaintiffs, it is essential that the insurance company believes throughout the litigation that you and your lawyers are willing to try the case before a jury. Why? Because insurance companies don't like when other people

At Shannon Law Group, our motto is, "WE WON'T FILE A CASE IF WE'RE NOT WILLING TO TRY IT."

(juries) tell them how much money they have to pay. Insurance is all about risk assessment and risk limitation. They don't like the uncertainties involved in a trial – that a jury might love the plaintiff, that a jury might hate the conduct of a defendant trucking company, etc. For these reasons if you have a good case, the closer a case gets to trial, the better the insurance company offers tend to be for an injured client.

You will likely be asked to testify at your trial. In order to understand how your injuries have affected your life, a jury needs to hear it from "the horse's mouth." Your attorney will ask you about any hobbies or activities that are negatively affected by your injuries. There may be some activities that you can no longer participate after your crash. Over the years, we have had clients testify about all sorts of hobbies that they can no longer do – gardening, exercising, golfing, arts and crafts, hiking, fishing, and the list goes on.

No matter your hobby, jurors understand the loss associated from not being able to do something that you loved. The beauty of trials is that the people evaluating your case have their own passions and experiences. They can put themselves in your shoes to appreciate your loss. An avid cyclist in the jury box may have never gardened in his life, but he knows how much less fulfilling his life would be if he could no longer participate in his beloved sport.

In addition, your attorney will ask you about how your injuries affect your daily activities that we take for granted every day – things like carrying grocery bags in from the car, climbing stairs, playing soccer with your kids, or walking the dog without pain.

If your case goes to trial, you should expect to be in attendance every day of the trial (absent extenuating circumstances). A jury will be asked to take days, sometimes weeks away from their jobs and families. It's a huge sacrifice for someone to sit on a jury in a serious injury case. It's why you often hear about people trying to skip out on their jury duty. The jury needs to understand that your serious injury case is worth their time. If your trial is not important enough for you to attend every day, a jury may agree with you. That undoubtedly yields a less than favorable result for your case.

Your attorney may request your spouse, other members of your family and/or friends to testify at trial. Oftentimes, the most compelling testimony regarding how an injury affects a person doesn't come from the injured plaintiff, but rather from someone close to them, who sees them every day, and can explain the struggles they witness from an outsider's perspective.

Ultimately, you should not be nervous about going to trial. It's an opportunity. If you're at trial, it's likely that the trucking company and its insurance company don't understand the gravity of your losses resulting from your crash. A trial is your one chance to show them.

RESOLUTION

Ultimately, every case we have is resolved either by jury verdict or settlement. Even if a case has resulted in a jury verdict and judgment against the trucking company, the case may still end up being resolved via settlement. Why? After a verdict for an injured victim, trucking companies will often appeal the result alleging that some problem at trial prevented them from receiving a fair trial. Appeals can take several years from verdict to appellate decision. Accordingly, an appealing trucking insurer may decide to try to settle a case post-verdict to avoid incurring additional attorney's fees and so that you don't have to wait more time to get paid.

Once a case is resolved by jury verdict or settlement, your lawyers have additional work to do to ensure that the most amount of money as possible ends up in your pocket. The most important thing your lawyers have to do, once a case against a trucking company has been settled, is to resolve any outstanding liens. Your lawyers will explain to you in far greater detail what liens are and how they affect your recovery, but the abridged version is this: liens are claims against settlement proceeds made by entities that have paid money or provided services to you as a result of the injuries sustained in the crash. Most often, these lien claims are made by healthcare providers and health insurers that may have paid some of your medical bills.

CONCLUSION

The above timeline provides a mere outline of what a typical trucking case might look like. As with everything else in life, a trucking case's timeline can be highly variable based on your attorneys, your health, opposing attorneys, treating medical personnel, and the judge assigned to move your case along. At our firm, we strive to push your case to trial as quickly as we can, and we will not hesitate in using the court to help us do so. If you ever have questions about what's going on in your case or what you can expect coming down the pipeline, a good trucking attorney will have no problem answering any such questions for you.

CHAPTER 7

HOW DO I SURVIVE WHILE MY CASE IS PENDING?

E very person that walks through our firm's door has a role in their family's economy. Sometimes they are the family's primary breadwinner. Sometimes they are the family member charged with the great task of maintaining the household – making sure there are groceries in the pantry, that the kids get to practice on time, and the hundreds of other things required to keep the family engine running smoothly. Sometimes they are living on their own doing their best to earn a good living. When an individual can't fulfill their role, the family's economy is crushed. Often, a catastrophic injury that leaves someone unable to work or unable to maintain his or her household delivers a crushing blow not just to the injured victim, but to the entire family.

Most of the families that come into our office after a catastrophic crash have already incurred a mountain of medical bills. Many of them expect the at-fault trucking company's insurer to pay for all their medical bills as they are incurred. Unfortunately, that's not how the system has been set up. A bad driver's insurance company won't pay anything until the case is completely over through settlement or trial verdict. In Cook County, where most of our cases are filed, that can mean years of medical bills accruing before the trucking insurer pays anything.

OPTIONS TO HELP YOUR SURVIVE FINANCIALLY

MEDICAL PAYMENTS COVERAGE

If you maintain auto insurance (which you should), you likely have medical payments coverage under your policy – unless you expressly refused the coverage. Under your medical payment ("MedPay") coverage, your auto insurer will help pay crash-related medical bills up to the limits of your MedPay coverage. Look at your insurance policy's declaration page to determine the amount of your MedPay. Your attorney will submit your medical bills to your insurer and they (assuming they operate the way they are supposed to) will issue a check to you for the amount of the bills up to the policy limits. At the end of your case, your auto insurer will want to recover some of the money that they paid out towards your bills. Consider it a loan to help you survive until the time comes for the bad driver's insurer to pay. Here's a tip: Buy at least $50,000 in MedPay coverage for your policy. It could help a lot down the line.

State Farm Mutual Automobile Insurance Company

2702 Ireland Grove Rd
Bloomington IL 61709

NAMED INSURED
AT2
13-1969-55II   A

90185-5-I   MUTL   VOL

DECLARATIONS PAGE

POLICY NUMBER
POLICY PERIOD J   0
12:01 A.M. Standard Time

AGENT

DO NOT PAY PREMIUMS SHOWN ON THIS PAGE.
IF AN AMOUNT IS DUE, THEN A SEPARATE STATEMENT IS ENCLOSED.

YOUR CAR

YEAR	MAKE	MODEL	BODY STYLE	VEHICLE ID. NUMBER	CLASS

SYMBOLS	COVERAGE & LIMITS	PREMIUMS
A	Liability Coverage Bodily Injury Limits Each Person, Each Accident $100,000 $300,000 Property Damage Limit Each Accident $100,000	$194.80
C	Medical Payments Coverage Limit - Each Person $5,000	$14.67
D	Comprehensive Coverage - $500 Deductible	$26.01
G	Collision Coverage - $500 Deductible	$123.29
H	Emergency Road Service Coverage	$3.40
R1	Car Rental and Travel Expenses Coverage Limit - Car Rental Expense Each Day, Each Loss $25 $600	$10.40
U	Uninsured Motor Vehicle Coverage Bodily Injury Limits Each Person, Each Accident $100,000 $300,000	$8.15
W	Underinsured Motor Vehicle Coverage Bodily Injury Limits Each Person, Each Accident $100,000 $300,000	$8.32

ENSURE MEDICAL PROVIDERS BILL Y OUR HEALTH INSURER

There's a reason that you pay your monthly health insurance premiums – to protect yourself from huge medical expenses as a result of trauma such as a truck crash. Sometimes medical providers, who have agreements in place with most health insurers, try to avoid submitting your bills to your insurer because they believe they can recover more money from the proceeds of a settlement.

To the best of your ability, don't let the insurance companies get away with it. If the hospital refuses to submit your bills to your health insurance company, we're happy to talk with them. Oftentimes, we can illustrate to them that processing your bills through your own health insurance is in the hospital's own best interest.

CHECK YOUR ELIGIBILITY FOR ASSISTANCE PROGRAMS

As an injured victim, there may be several public and private assistance programs that can help you endure the difficult financial situations that lie ahead. In the past, we've had clients that have successfully applied for Medicare, Medicaid, Social Security Disability benefits, short-term and long-term disability insurance benefits, and unemployment benefits, among others. Talk to your lawyer about your potential eligibility for any of these programs.

In addition to the above-listed programs, our clients have worked with some great local charity organizations that help people in need. If you need assistance, talk with us about what you need, and we will do our best to connect you to the organization best suited for your needs.

CHAPTER 8

CONCLUSION

I f you are reading this book, it's likely because you or someone close to you has been severely injured in a trucking crash or other truck-related accident. Having seen dozens of families cope with devastating injuries caused by the negligence of trucking companies, I recognize that you are going through an extremely stressful and difficult time. Hopefully this book provided you with some broad brush strokes about what to expect in pursuing your lawsuit. Obviously, one book cannot come close to providing all of the answers that you have about the unfamiliar road ahead.

If you take just one thing away from this book, let it be this – make sure to hire an attorney that you trust will be able to come through for you. At our firm, we try to deliver the highest quality legal representation with an unrivaled level of compassion for our clients. Our goal is not to represent a client on a transactional basis for their one case. We want to be the attorneys that you call for the rest of your life, whenever you have a legal issue.

APPENDIX A:

TRUCKING CRASH STATISTICS

NATIONAL STATISTICS

According to the U.S. Department of Transportation, there are hundreds of thousands of crashes involving large trucks or buses. In 2017 alone, states reported 171,140 crashes involving large trucks – 5,123 of which involved a fatality and 93,326 of which involved injuries of some kind.[3] In 2018, truck crashes as a whole increased to over 180,000, but fortunately crashes involving a fatality fell slightly. These numbers reflect only the crashes that were properly reported to federal agencies. We have had several cases in which the motor carrier involved in a serious accident never bothered to inform the DOT despite their obligation to do so.

If you've ever driven on Interstate 80 or Interstate 55 near Chicago, you understand just how many trucks are on the

---

3   U.S.D.O.T. Federal Motor Carrier Safety Administration, Motor Carrier Safety Progress Report – 6.30.19.

road today.[4] In 2016, there were over eleven million registered trucks in the United States. Those eleven million trucks, driven by over six million truck drivers, traveled a total of ***288 billion vehicle miles*** in 2016 alone.

Usually when a truck is involved in a crash, investigating officers perform a DOT inspection of the driver and the vehicle. These inspections determine whether the driver, the motor carrier, and the vehicle involved in the crash are in compliance with the Federal Motor Carrier Safety Regulations. Violations can be severe enough that the authorized safety inspector can actually order the driver or vehicle "out of service" until the violation is remedied.

In 2017, approximately 5% of all inspections resulted in a driver being ordered out of service. Given that more than 3,000,000 inspections were conducted that year, the 5% figure represents 150,000 unsafe truck drivers and is an alarming sign that many motor carriers are not doing enough to ensure compliance with the safety rules. Among the most frequent driver violations are logbook violations, speeding, disobeying the hours of service requirements (limiting the number of hours a driver can be on the road), and failing to obey traffic control devices.

ILLINOIS STATISTICS

In Illinois, tractor-trailer crashes make up only 3.5% of all crashes, but nearly 10% of all fatalities, highlighting the inherent dangers of operating large rigs.[5] In total, there were over 11,000 crashes involving tractor-trailers. Over 1,800 of those crashes involved some type of injury.

---

4   U.S.D.O.T. Federal Motor Carrier Safety Administration, 2018 Pocket Guide to Large Truck and Bus Statistics.
5   I.D.O.T. 2017 Illinois Crash Facts and Statistics (May 2019).

Fortunately for Illinois drivers, crashes involving fatalities in Illinois trail the national average significantly. With Chicago being far and away the largest population center in Illinois, it is not surprising that approximately 25% of all serious injury or fatality crashes occur in Cook County. Less obvious is why Will County consistently ranks as the county with the second highest number of fatalities or serious injuries every year. There are likely various reasons why Will County sees so many dangerous collisions, but you can't ignore that Interstate 80 and Interstate 55 traverse the county with trucks from all across the country accessing the massive Chicago market.

COMMON CAUSES OF TRUCKING CRASHES

When the Federal Motor Carrier Safety Administration investigates serious truck crashes, they will identify the critical cause of the crash. To do so, they break down causes into three major categories: driver, vehicle, and environment.

Of the driver causes, the FMCSA further breaks down causes into four sub-categories: Non-performance (when a driver falls asleep or is disabled by a heart attack or seizure), Recognition (when a driver is inattentive or distracted, or when he fails to observe potential hazards in time), Decision (when a driver makes an error in decision making by following too closely or driving too fast for conditions), and Performance (when a driver fails to exercise control over his vehicle, whether he's panicking or overcompensating).

Approximately 87% of all truck crashes are determined to be caused by driver error. On the other side of the spectrum, only 3% of crashes are attributable to weather or road conditions. We know that many crashes occur in snowy, rainy, or dark conditions. So wouldn't every one of those crashes be coded as an environmental cause? Not exactly. That's because the Federal Motor Carrier Safety Regulations require truck drivers to *recognize* dangerous weather conditions, and if necessary, pull over to the side of the road to wait out the dangerous condition. For that reason, a lot of weather-related crashes are attributed to the truck driver's failure to recognize the dangerous conditions prior to the crash.

APPENDIX B

FREQUENTLY ASKED QUESTIONS ABOUT TRUCKING CASES

HOW DO I PAY MY MEDICAL BILLS?

Unfortunately, trucking companies and their insurers will not pay your medical bills as they come in. A defendant insurance company will only write a check to cover medical expenses at the END of the case – whether by settlement or jury verdict. More information on alternative methods to help you with your medical bills can be found in Chapter 7.

HOW LONG DOES THIS ENTIRE PROCESS TAKE?

It depends. Though it may not seem like a particularly helpful answer, it's the truth. Some firms advertise that they will have your case settled in "x" amount of days guaranteed. Those firms typically settle their client's cases for pennies on the dollar. On the other hand, our firm has one and only one goal in mind: to net you the most amount of money as possible. Obviously, we try to move your case through the system as quickly as we can. However, we make sure that we conduct a thorough investigation and discovery process, crossing all of our "T"s and dotting all of our "I"s. Sometimes that can take time, often due to the roadblocks put in front of us by insurance companies. In our experience, though, having the patience necessary to properly build a trucking case against a company will all of the resources in the world is worth the wait.

SHOULD I TALK TO THE INSURANCE COMPANIES?

No. While insurance companies hold themselves out as being "friendly neighbors" and keeping you "in good hands," the reality is that they are in the litigation business. Their job isn't to help you or pay you the fair value on your claim. It's to keep the most amount of money as possible in their hands and out of yours.

Whenever an insurance company contacts you to discuss your case, a red flag should go up. If it's the trucking company's insurer, direct them to your attorneys immediately. You have no obligation to discuss your case or your injuries with them. If it's your own insurance company, you should probably still direct them to your lawyer. If nothing else, your attorney can be on the telephone with you as you discuss medical payment coverage or getting money for your totaled vehicle with your insurance company.

DOES WHICH ATTORNEY I HIRE ACTUALLY MATTER?

Absolutely yes. Hiring an attorney without the required specialized knowledge and experience can cripple even the best case. Our client, Bethany, recently came to our office about six months after she had hired another firm that held themselves out to be competent trucking lawyers. She complained to us that she never received responses to any of her calls or emails to her lawyers. In the six months since these lawyers signed up the case, they had not done a thing to move the case forward – no investigation, no procuring medical records, nothing. The former attorneys told our client that they were waiting for her to finish medical treatment before they would start to work up her case.

Unfortunately for Bethany, all her previous attorneys had done was give the insurance company a massive head start in preparing the case for trial. Within a month of hiring us, we requested all of her medical records and bills, hired an investigator to obtain witness statements, subpoenaed the Illinois State Police for their entire investigation file (including video footage taken from inside the truck driver's cab), and put her case in suit.

In Bethany's case, she was able to find good lawyers in time to fix the mistakes of the lawyers she hired originally. Other folks that have come through our door over the years have not been so lucky.

Hiring an attorney without the required specialized knowledge and experience can cripple even the best case.

WHAT SHOULD I LOOK FOR IN A LAWYER?

Generally speaking, a good trucking lawyer should be able to (1) promptly investigate your case, (2) guide you through every aspect of the lawsuit; (3) discuss your options and make reasoned recommendations; and (4) build and improve the value of your case.

More important than any of those things, a good trucking lawyer is someone who you can trust. If you meet with an attorney and do not trust that he or she is willing to fight for your case competently and ethically, it's time to continue your search.

WHAT IS A DEPOSITION?

A deposition is an oral testimony taken under oath before a trial or arbitration. It is customary that depositions be taken of the parties to a lawsuit. Often depositions are also taken of witnesses and others who might testify at trial, including family members. Even though it often takes place in a conference room or office, and the setting is somewhat informal, it is a very important event in any lawsuit.

The questions you will be asked pertain to information relevant to your trucking accident case. For example, you will be asked about your medical, employment and educational background, and about the crash and your injuries.

Prior to your deposition, your attorney will meet with you to prepare you. In a typical preparation meeting, your attorney will explain the types of questions you may be asked, the rules of depositions, what to wear, etc. In many cases, your attorney may put you through a mock cross examination, so you are more comfortable when the insurance company lawyer asks you questions at the deposition. The most important thing to know for a deposition: Tell the truth. An injured victim's deposition will never, by itself, win a trucking crash case. But, if an individual plays fast and easy with the facts of the crash, or greatly exaggerates his injuries, it can be a catastrophic blow to your case.

HOW LONG DO I HAVE TO FILE MY CASE?

The answer to this question varies considerably depending on the type of case, the jurisdiction, and the potential negligent defendants. In Illinois, for example, most victims injured in a trucking crash have two (2) years from the date of the crash to file a lawsuit against the trucking company. However, there are exceptions. Say, for example, the negligent driver was an employee of a municipality of government agency. Many government entities have immunities that limit the amount of time you have to sue them after an accident.

Additionally, in many other states, you have an obligation to notify the defendants of a potential lawsuit well in advance of filing the lawsuit. In some cases, we have seen notice rules that require an injured victim to notify defendants of a potential lawsuit as quickly as ninety days after your injury.

All of this is to say that if you are injured in a trucking crash (or really any type of accident in which someone was negligent), it's important to consult an attorney ASAP to learn your rights and obligations for filing your lawsuit.

I MAY HAVE SOME OF THE BLAME IN THIS CRASH – HOW DOES IT AFFECT MY CASE?

Sometimes our clients feel some guilt that their actions may have contributed in some way to their injuries. In Illinois, we have what's called a modified comparative fault rule. What that means is that at trial, a jury will determine whether you have any responsibility for the accident. If they determine that your actions contributed to the crash, they will apportion how much responsibility your bear vs. the truck driver.

If a jury determines that you bore no responsibility for your crash, you would be entitled to all of the damages that the jury awards. If the jury determines that you were 10% responsible for your crash, the judge would reduce the total damages awarded by the jury by 10%. The giant caveat under Illinois law: If a jury determines that you're *more than* 50% responsible for your own crash, you are not entitled to recover anything against the other driver.

THE TRUCK DRIVER'S INSURANCE COMPANY "ADMITTED FAULT" – SHOULD I SETTLE?

No. First off, an insurance claim adjuster's assertion that the company has "admitted fault" means nothing. It may or may not be true, and it's not binding in court. Nothing prevents the insurance company from telling you that it's admitting fault all while getting admissions from you that they can use to dispute fault later on.

Second, in the exceedingly rare scenario in which a trucking insurance company is accepting responsibility for their conduct, the insurance company will not be offering you close to what your case is worth. "Admitting fault" when talking to an injured victim is part of the insurance company playbook on how to resolve cases early (for pennies on the dollar) before you hire an attorney who understands what your case is actually worth.

I CAN'T GO BACK TO MY OLD JOB – HOW DOES THAT FACTOR INTO MY CASE?

If the injuries from your crash render you unable to return your previous job on a temporary or permanent basis, you may be able to recover those lost wages from the trucking company and their insurer.

In cases when you can no longer return to your old job, your attorney will likely hire an economist to assess the financial damages you have suffered as a result of these injuries. To do so, she will evaluate the earning capacity you had in your previous job and compare it to the earning capacity you now have given your physical limitations. The difference in those two figures represents what's known as your "lost earning capacity." For more information on what damages may be available to you, check out Chapter 4.

ABOUT THE AUTHOR

PATRICK CUMMINGS

PATRICK CUMMINGS is a Chicago attorney who represents individuals who have been harmed by the negligence or recklessness of others. Pat focuses his practice on helping people who have suffered significant and life-altering injuries – often in truck or motor vehicle crashes.

For his entire legal career, Pat has represented people that have been harmed by others; often this involves taking on large corporations and insurance companies. While defense firms and insurance companies may view litigation as simply a cost of doing business, Patrick understands that each case in our office matters tremendously to each client.

Most of the time, Pat is representing individuals in a time of crisis in their life who have no experience with the civil justice system. At Shannon Law Group, we relish the opportunity to work with these great clients, shoulder the burden of dealing with courts and insurance companies, and obtain positive results for our clients.

Patrick has handled a number of trucking cases from initial intake through final resolution of the case. He has taken hundreds of depositions, settled many six-and-seven figure cases and tried several cases to jury verdict. In his first solo jury trial, Patrick secured a jury verdict for his client that was over ten times the insurance company's final offer to the client. In each of the past few years, Patrick has secured for his clients some of the top trucking-related settlements in the state.

Patrick resides in Chicago with his wife, Caitlin, where they are parishioners at St. Alphonsus in Lakeview. When he's not in the office, you may find Pat woodworking, playing a round of golf, or supporting his Marquette Golden Eagles basketball team.

Shannon Law Group

A Professional Corporation

Chicago Office
135 S. LaSalle, Suite 2200
Chicago, Illinois 60603

Woodridge Office
3550 Hobson Road, Suite 403
Woodridge, Illinois 60517

www.shannonlawgroup.com
Tel. 312.578.9501
Fax. 312.268.5474
Email: pcummings@shannonlawgroup.com

WA